Who On Earth is Aldo Leopold?

Father of Wildlife Ecology

Read about other Scientists Saving the Earth

Who on Earth is Aldo Leopold?
Father of Wildlife Ecology
ISBN-13: 978-1-59845-115-3
ISBN-10:   1-59845-115-4

Who on Earth is Archie Carr?
Protector of Sea Turtles
ISBN-13: 978-1-59845-120-7
ISBN-10:   1-59845-120-0

Who on Earth is Rachel Carson?
Mother of the Environmental Movement
ISBN-13: 978-1-59845-116-0
ISBN-10:   1-59845-116-2

Who on Earth is Sylvia Earle?
Undersea Explorer of the Ocean
ISBN-13: 978-1-59845-118-4
ISBN-10:   1-59845-118-9

Who on Earth is Dian Fossey?
Defender of the Mountain Gorillas
ISBN-13: 978-1-59845-117-7
ISBN-10:   1-59845-117-0

Who on Earth is Jane Goodall?
Champion for the Chimpanzees
ISBN-13: 978-1-59845-119-1
ISBN-10:   1-59845-119-7

Scientists Saving the Earth

Who On Earth is Aldo Leopold?
Father of Wildlife Ecology

Marty Fletcher and Glenn Scherer

Enslow Publishers, Inc.
40 Industrial Road
Box 398
Berkeley Heights, NJ 07922
USA
http://www.enslow.com

Library of Congress Cataloging-in-Publication Data

Scherer, Glenn.
 Who on earth is Aldo Leopold?: father of wildlife ecology / Glenn Scherer and Marty Fletcher.
     p. cm.—(Scientists saving the earth)
 Includes bibliographical references and index.
 Summary: "Details the life of Aldo Leopold, with chapters devoted to his early years, life, work,
ecological writings, and legacy, as well as how children can follow in his footsteps"—Provided
by publisher.
 ISBN-13: 978-1-59845-115-3 (hardcover)
 ISBN-10: 1-59845-115-4 (hardcover)
 1. Leopold, Aldo, 1886-1948—Juvenile literature. 2. Ecologists—United States—
Biography—Juvenile literature. 3. Wildlife managers—United States—Biography—
Juvenile literature. 4. Foresters—United States—Biography—Juvenile literature.
I.
Fletcher, Marty. II. Title.
 QH31.L618S34 2010
 577.092—dc22
 [B]

                              2008010295

Printed in the United States of America

10 9 8 7 6 5 4 3 2 1

To Our Readers:
We have done our best to make sure all Internet Addresses in this book were active and appropriate
when we went to press. However, the author and the publisher have no control over and assume no
liability for the material available on those Internet sites or on other Web sites they may link to. Any
comments or suggestions can be sent by e-mail to comments@enslow.com or to the address on the
back cover.

♻ Enslow Publishers, Inc., is committed to printing our books on recycled paper. The paper in every
book contains 10% to 30% post-consumer waste (PCW). The cover board on the outside of each book
contains 100% PCW. Our goal is to do our part to help young people and the environment too!

Photo Credits: © The Aldo Leopold Foundation: pp. 30, 43, 80, 93;Courtesy of Daderot on
Wikimedia: p. 27; Courtesy of Megan Longcor: pp. 88–89;Courtesy of the University of Wisconsin—
Madison Archives: pp. 20, 23, 45; © Enslow Publishers, Inc., p. 19 (bottom);Franklin Delano
Roosevelt Presidential Library: pp. 64, 69, 75, Library of Congress: pp. 35, 49, 66, 70; © Shutterstock:
pp. 6–7, 10–11, 19, 34, 40–41, 44, 50–51, 53, 57, 95; © U.S. Department of Defense: pp. 55, 78; ©
Wisconsin Historical Society: pp. iii, 13.

Cover Photo: Credit: Fred Ludekens: Courtesy of the Weyerhaeuser Archives

Contents

1

Aldo Leopold dedicated his life to preserving America's natural habitat so that everyone—people or animals—could enjoy it.

Learning to Think Like a Mountain

In the early 1900s, when Aldo Leopold was a young man, he worked as a forester in the Apache National Forest in east-central Arizona. It was his job to help protect thousands of acres of woods from fire. He also helped manage the grasslands where sheep, cattle, and other livestock grazed for food. In addition, he helped make sure that the national forest produced a large quantity of game animals, such as wild deer and elk, for hunters to shoot.

At that time, everyone believed that the best way to produce more deer, elk, and other game animals that hunters stalked was to kill any animal that killed them—especially wolves.

For hundreds of years, Americans had waged war on wolves, and with seeming good reason. In colonial America, which was built on a delicate livestock economy, just surviving had been a challenge. Settlers who lost even a few calves to a pack of wolves could starve, losing their livelihoods and their farms. For that reason, large rewards had been placed on wolves. During the 1830s in Tennessee, a wolf pelt turned over to the authorities could be worth as much as three dollars, equal to roughly $70 today. Not surprisingly, such bounties resulted in the slaughter of wolves; by 1900, they had been virtually eliminated in the eastern United States, and very few remained in the West, even in remote places like Apache National Forest. This unfortunate attitude hadn't changed much in the early years of the twentieth century, and most people still seemed to think that the only good wolf was a dead wolf.

Encounter With an Old Wolf

Like most people in Arizona at the time, Aldo Leopold was happy to kill wolves—until one day when an old wolf taught him a new and important lesson.

On this particular day, Leopold and his fellow foresters were eating lunch on a rocky ridge. At the bottom of the ridge flowed a fast-moving river. As the men ate, they watched what they thought was a large deer crossing the stream. But when the animal reached the near side of the river and shook itself dry, they were shocked to realize that it was a large old wolf. As the wolf came ashore, a half dozen young, yelping wolf pups ran out of the cover of some willow trees to greet their mother. Remembering the event years later, Leopold wrote:

In these days we had never heard of passing up a chance to kill a wolf. In a second we were pumping lead into the pack. . . . When our rifles were empty, the old wolf was down. . . . We reached the old wolf in time to watch a fierce green fire dying in her eyes. I realized then, and have known since, that there was something new to me in those eyes—something known only to her and to the mountain. I was young then, and full of trigger-itch; I thought that because fewer wolves meant more deer, that no wolves would mean hunters' paradise. But after seeing the green fire die, I sensed that neither the wolf nor the mountain agreed with such a view.[1]

In *A Sand County Almanac,* Leopold goes on to explain what happens when all wolves, or any other large predator, are eliminated from a habitat. Not only is something magnificent lost, but without wolves and other big predators, deer and

Leopold's experience hunting a wolf in the early twentieth century in Arizona's Apache National Forest taught him the importance of respecting nature and everything in it.

some omnivores begin to reproduce out of control. Their numbers soar, and soon they eat the leaves off every tree and bush. Eventually the deer population becomes so large and they eat so much that they run out of food and begin to starve to death.

The scientific truth that Aldo Leopold learned that day—that the elimination of one "problem" species leads to other, unanticipated problems—has been proved again and again across the American West. For example, the systematic destruction of more than six thousand large predators, including wolves, cougars, coyotes, and bobcats, in the Kaibab game preserve on the north rim of the Grand Canyon in the early twentieth century resulted in the utter ruin of this reserve. Without predators to keep deer populations in check, the number of deer exploded from just four thousand to one hundred thousand. The starving animals died by the thousands, and soon "[t]he whole country looked as though a swarm of locusts had swept through it, leaving the range . . . torn, gray, stripped, and dying."[2]

Wolves, wrote Leopold, must survive in order for the mountain ecosystem of the U.S. Southwest to survive. Just as important, he contended, wolves should be preserved for their own sake. They have a right to live and roam the earth, just as much as human beings. This was a very new idea in the early twentieth century.

⊙ Leopold learned early in his life that all aspects of nature have value and that people must learn to coexist with it, not try to dominate it.

Ultimately, Leopold also saw "the fierce green fire" in the old wolf's eyes as a symbol for all wild creatures and all wildlands. He recognized that human beings cannot live without the "the fierce green fire" of the wild, and that when we destroy animals or ecosystems, we are actually destroying a little bit of ourselves.

Teaching the World About the Value of Wildness

The day he shot the old wolf, Leopold learned that wildness and wilderness must not be destroyed, that each has a tremendous value in and of itself. It is a great lesson that he later taught to America and the world in his groundbreaking book *A Sand County Almanac,* completed in 1948. Had he never written that book, Aldo Leopold's name and work might be mostly forgotten today. Because of that single but very important book, he is considered by many historians to be the first great wildlife ecologist, and one of the founders of the modern environmental movement.

Because of Aldo Leopold and some other visionary thinkers, wolves, mountain lions, grizzly bears, and other once-despised predators have come to be appreciated. Likewise, once-hated landscapes like mangrove swamps, deserts, and grasslands have also come to be valued, not just for the natural resources they provide, but for the one-of-a-kind plants and animals that grow there and for the way their ecosystems make our lives better.

A Still Controversial Idea

Leopold's belief that all plants and animals in an ecosystem are valuable and have a right to exist for their own sake is still controversial.

For example, while many people want to strengthen the U.S. Endangered Species Act to protect more plants and animals around our nation, still others want to weaken the act to protect fewer species. Passed in 1973, the act protects species from extinction as a result of man-made activities, such as development. Likewise, while some people want to better protect wolves, cougars, grizzly bears and the habitats in which they roam, others want to mine, log, drill, and otherwise utilize those wild lands to meet human needs for natural resources.

While some people want to protect all wild things, there are still some who imagine that the best way to promote the growth of game herds is to kill all big predators. This conflict boiled over in Alaska as recently as 2007, when the state government issued a $150 bounty for every wolf that could be shot from an airplane by private pilots, supposedly in order to help boost the moose and elk population. (The program was stopped after a judge issued a restraining order.)[3]

In one of his essays, Leopold warned against such practices, saying, "You cannot love game and hate predators. . . . The land is one organism."[4] In other words, the wholesale destruction of Alaskan wolves would, according to the ecological science pioneered by Leopold, result in overgrazing, ruining plant growth, and possibly lead to the collapse of the ecosystem.

The controversial conservation ideas that Leopold first expressed in *A Sand County Almanac* continue to form a cornerstone of environmental thinking today. And Leopold is seen by many environmentalists as one of the great scientists saving the earth.

The Early Years

Aldo Leopold was born in Burlington, Iowa, a small city on the Mississippi River, on January 11, 1887. At that time, Burlington and its surroundings were still semi-wild. Just fifty years earlier, the town had been a frontier outpost. It was a place that the Sac, Sauk, and Fox Indian tribes that lived in the area had called Shok-Ko-Kon, meaning "the flint hills," because the area contained a great deal of chert, a stone used to make arrowheads.

When Leopold was three years old, the American frontier was finally and officially declared closed by the U.S. government. This meant that the country was now settled, and that there was no more unexplored wilderness in the continental United States; towns and farms stretched from coast to coast, and the age of exploration and pioneering was officially over.

Man vs. Wild

The result was that Leopold grew up in a time and place of amazing contrasts. Burlington, Iowa, was still fairly wild, with dense and mysterious woodland inhabited by game birds, rabbits, and other animals. It was also a place that was developing quickly with roads, railroad tracks, and town life encroaching on the countryside. The famous writer Mark Twain in his book *Life on the Mississippi* may have described the region's natural and human contrasts best:

The majestic bluffs that overlook the [Mississippi] river along through this region charm one with the grace and variety of their forms and the soft beauty of their [natural] adornment. . . . And it is all as tranquil and reposeful as dreamland, and has nothing this-worldly about it—nothing to hang a fret or worry upon. . . . Until the unholy train comes tearing along—which it presently does, ripping the sacred solitude to rags and tatters with the devil's war whoop and the roar and the thunder of its rushing wheels—and straightway you are back in this [civilized] world. . . .

The Mississippi River near Burlington, Iowa.

Leopold spent his childhood in this environment of receding wilderness and advancing civilization. His experience watching wildlands being overrun by development would have a big influence on his future career and ecological ideas.

A Happy Family

Aldo Leopold was the oldest of four children born to Carl and Clara Leopold. Aldo's sister, Marie, was born in 1888; his brother Carl Jr. came along in 1892, and Frederic in 1895. Aldo got along well with his brothers and sister, and they all played together in the woods around Burlington.

Aldo lived with his parents and grandparents in a small mansion on Prospect Hill, one of the bluffs of the flint hills. Aldo's father ran a company that made fine desks, from hardwoods harvested from the region. The family's house had a spectacular view of the Mississippi River and many miles of river valley floodplain. Each fall and spring, the Leopolds were treated to a spectacular display of birds migrating north or south along the river. Steamboats with their passengers and cargoes of logs, lumber,

Aldo Leopold as a child.

tools, and agricultural crops were a constant on the huge Mississippi.

Learning From His GrandFather

Aldo was close to both his parents and his grand-parents, Charles and Marie Runge Starker. Grandfather Charles was an architect, an amateur naturalist, and a man with vision. He convinced Burlington city politicians to buy up some of the town's last wildlands to serve as open space for wildlife and as a place for people to hike and picnic. The park still exists. It is known as Crapo Park, and in the middle is Starker Lake, named for Aldo's grandfather.

Leopold's grandfather also revived the land around the family house. He planted a vegetable garden, formal flower gardens, pine, oak, maple, and fruit trees. He enlisted the help of his entire family and it is obvious that young Aldo learned a great deal from the experience—years later, he would buy a run down farm in Wisconsin and do to it what his grandfather had done in Iowa. Aldo Leopold's experience in Wisconsin became *A Sand County Almanac,* the book that helped kick-start the environmental movement.

An Avid Outdoorsman

When he was young, Leopold rambled along the bluffs and bottomlands of the Mississippi River.

His grandparents and parents were amateur naturalists and sportsmen, and he learned a great deal about nature from the four of them. Aldo's mother was an expert skater and taught her children to love winter sports. Aldo's father took his children for hikes as soon as they were able. Carl would quiz the children about everything they saw as they walked.

"He would open up a decaying hollow log to show us the life dwelling inside, such as mice or large insects," remembered Aldo's brother Frederic years later. "He might show where a mink had dug into a muskrat house to kill himself a muskrat for dinner. He pointed out the old raccoon droppings, which might be identified by the content of wild grape seeds. We did not need to kill game to have an exciting afternoon in the swamp or field."[1]

Aldo soon became an avid birder, hunter, and fisherman. "He was very much an outdoorsman," recalled his sister, Marie, "even in his extreme youth. He was always out climbing around the bluffs, or going down to the river, or going across the river into the woods."[2]

Hunter, Conservationist, and Ornithologist

By the time he was eleven years old, Aldo had already learned to move like a hunter—quietly

Aldo Leopold (standing, left) with his mother, brothers, and sister.

and deliberately. And he put those skills to good use, hunting quail and ducks and other game through prairie, oak-hickory forest, and down ravines leading to the Mississippi. From his father, Aldo learned a conservationist's ethic: He did not shoot more game than he needed to feed his family, even though there were no laws limiting the number of animals a hunter could kill. Aldo never shot animals just for the sport of killing them. And if he wounded an animal, but did not kill it, he would track it down rather than allow it to suffer. His father even taught Aldo to stop hunting a species of animal if it seemed the animal was becoming scarce—the Leopolds knew the species needed time to reproduce, replenish, and recover. And though it was legal to hunt anytime back then, Carl never hunted in the spring because that was when most animals had their babies.

Carl Leopold's conservationist thinking was unusual for the time. Many Americans believed that game was limitless and could survive the relentless slaughter. For example, market hunters, who hunted wild game to sell to the public, would kill thousands of ducks in a single season, causing a severe decrease in game species. Market hunters were so thorough that they made a species like the passenger pigeon extinct. In the early 1800s, passenger pigeons were so abundant that flocks could block out the sun and seemingly turn day into night. But by 1900, hunters had driven the species to extinction in the wild; the last passenger pigeon died in captivity in 1909. These realities were not lost on Aldo Leopold.

Budding Naturalist

By the time he was a teenager, Leopold had become a capable ornithologist, a person who studies birds. He made careful drawings of the birds he saw and kept detailed notes about each new discovery. He would return to the same places every day to quietly study the same birds and their daily habits. Aldo's early journals, written neatly in a child's hand, were the first of thousands of pages of nature notes he would keep throughout his life. His ability to observe nature so closely, and to record what he saw, would be essential to the writing of *A Sand County Almanac*.

Studying Hard

Aldo loved nature, but he loved learning too. His home was filled with all kinds of books, and he read most of them. Not surprisingly, his favorite reading dealt with nature and the outdoors: His favorites were, *The Adventures of Daniel Boone*, books by Jack London (who wrote about Alaska), and his father's issues of *Outings* magazine.

Aldo attended elementary and high school in Burlington, Iowa. His high school was so crowded that he was only required to attend afternoon sessions. He made good use of his free time, exploring the woods and fields around Burlington and continuing his private nature studies. School helped him sharpen his skills in geography, science, history, and especially writing. Aldo's essays were known for the care with which they were written, and he also excelled in biology.

Aldo was an excellent student and it seemed that he would do well in almost any career he chose. Aldo's father hoped his oldest son would follow him into his own business and one day become president of the Leopold Desk Company. But Carl also noted that the shipments of pine he used to make his desks were becoming fewer and fewer—and without those logs, there would be no desks and no desk company. Carl realized Aldo might have a future working to try to protect and preserve nature, and in regrowing the nation's forests. He encouraged his son to pursue a career as a forester.

Aldo didn't need much encouragement. He quickly decided that a career in forestry was exactly what he wanted—doing so would allow him to continue his walks in the woods, his nature studies, and nature journals. What could be better?

A Career Presents Itself

Luckily, the United States government was just then realizing that it was in serious need of foresters. The country's forests had once been so vast that it was said that a squirrel could hop from the Atlantic Ocean to the Mississippi River without

This is the Edith Memorial Chapel on the Lawrenceville School campus. Aldo attended Lawrenceville School, a preparatory school in Lawrenceville, N.J.

ever touching the ground. Things were becoming very different by the late 1880s. Uncontrolled logging had destroyed the vast forests of the East and the West. An alarmed President Grover Cleveland appointed Gifford Pinchot to the National Forest Commission and gave him the assignment of restoring the nation's forests, especially in the West. As a first step, in 1900 Pinchot and fellow Yale University graduate Henry S. Graves started the Yale University School of Forestry (now known as the School of Forestry and Environmental Studies).

Leopold set his sights on a career in forestry and hoped to attend the new forestry program at Yale. His chances of being admitted seemed slim, however, so his parents sent him to the Lawrenceville School, a prestigious college preparatory school in Lawrenceville, New Jersey.

Go East, Young Man

In January 1904, Aldo boarded a train and headed east to school in Lawrenceville, New Jersey. He dove into his studies, committing himself to classes in English, history, German, algebra, Bible study, and composition. He was still most interested in nature. And when he discovered a work of the evolutionist Charles Darwin in the library, he described his thrill in a letter home. He also heard a lecture by an American Indian that left a great impression on him. "Nature is the gate to the Great Mystery,"[3] said the man.

Aldo wrote a speech that made the case for forest preservation, saying that the failure to do so would wreck "nature's balance" and result in "changes in climate [to] follow."[4] He cited Spain, once the most powerful country in the world, as an example, showing how Spain's loss of its mountain forests had caused the country's climate to become hotter and drier and to turn it into a blistering desert. Aldo asserted that the decline of Spain as a world power was caused partly by the mismanagement and destruction of its natural resources. "She was once the most powerful nation on earth . . . [a]nd now this same Spain lies blistering under the heat of a tropical sun, a rainless desert," he wrote.[5]

All the while he was a student in New Jersey, Aldo continued his activities as game hunter and nature enthusiast; he took a special interest in plants. Most important, he began to note the interrelationships between insects, plants, birds, and other animals. In so doing, he was exploring the web of creation, or what we know today as the science of ecology.

A Conservationist in New Jersey

Aldo continued to develop his skills as a conservationist while at Lawrenceville. For example, one

Over the course of his life, Leopold spent countless hours in the woods and mountains, observing, watching, and learning about nature. In this 1938 photo, he is shown near Chihuahua, Mexico.

day as he rambled in the New Jersey hills, he found a half-dead muskrat in a trap. He released the struggling animal. Farther along, he found a dead muskrat rotting in another trap. An angry Aldo removed both traps. Later, he found another trap with another dead muskrat. He took that trap too. "So you see I have the three traps on my hands, which of course I will by no means give back to the person who traps in the breeding season, and much less if he leaves the carcasses to rot,"[6] Aldo wrote to his parents.

Standing Up to Power

Leopold was also not afraid to confront authority when it came to matters of conservation. For example, the school regularly drained a pond on its property, a practice that made Aldo angry. He and a friend went to the drained pond and found many dying fish and tadpoles. When the pond was refilled, the boys restocked it with fish, and Aldo resolved to talk to the school's director to stop the pond from being drained again.[7]

Yet, the adolescent Leopold was a long way from becoming a full-fledged ecologist who understood the subtle relationships between people, plants, and animals. He still went into the woods with a shotgun under his arm. And it was with a sense of glee that he shot birds that he considered pests. Crows, sparrows, and even hawks were blasted whenever he saw them, in order to, as he saw it, better protect the songbirds that he valued. Though Aldo stopped shooting these birds while he was at Lawrenceville, it would be several years before he completely understood that crows, sparrows, and especially predators like hawks, are important to a healthy ecosystem and are best left undisturbed.

Yale Forestry School

In 1905, when he was eighteen, Leopold was admitted to Yale University. He entered Yale's new forestry school in 1906 and began his intense training as a member of the nation's first generation of foresters.

Yale, located in New Haven, Connecticut, did not offer Leopold many opportunities to go tramping in the woods. He was, therefore, almost forced to apply himself exclusively to his studies. Once enrolled in the forestry school, he buried himself in the thorny details of forest management, timber harvest science, lumbering, timber use, and plant taxonomy. However, the young Leopold stole time to read novels, poetry, and philosophy, and to escape to his beloved woods. But the seemingly endless book and laboratory work caused him to sometimes turn rebellious: "You sit four hours a week squinting through a microscope at a little drop of mud all full of wiggly bugs and things, and then draw pictures of them and label [them] with ungodly Latin names. . . . One cannot help wondering what the *Cyanophycens oscillatius* has to do with raising timber."[8]

Though he obviously did not appreciate it at the time, this education increased to Leopold's knowledge of natural history. Some years later, he would write that "there are two things that interest me: the relation of people to each other, and the relation of people to land."[9] In other words, even so tiny a species as the microscopic *Cyanophycens oscillatius* had value. Understanding the complexities of ecology meant developing an understanding of every species in an ecosystem—no matter how tiny or seemingly insignificant—and their relationship to one another.

Utilitarianism Versus Conservation

Leopold was a rebellious student in another way. While he considered himself to be practical, he was reluctant to view nature as a "resource," and he had a difficult time seeing a spectacular grove of oak or hickory trees in terms of "board feet" or finished furniture. In other words, when he looked at those oak and hickory trees, he saw oak and hickory trees, not their dollar value.

At one extreme, there was the straightforward philosophy of the head of the new United States Forestry Service, Gifford Pinchot, who believed

⬆Rather than protect a forest in Yosemite National Park, Gifford Pinchot favored building a dam along the Tuolumne River in northern California in order to provide water for residents of San Francisco. After a long battle, the dam, Hetch Hetchy, was finally built in 1923.

Gifford Pinchot, shown here in a photograph taken in 1925, was the first Chief of the U.S. Forest Service and helped establish the Yale University School of Forestry that Leopold attended.

that the nation's forests served as "a perpetual supply of timber for home industries. . . . "[10] Pinchot did not believe in protecting nature for nature's sake. He believed in managing nature so that its resources could be used by people. For example, rather than protect a spectacular forested valley in California called Hetch Hetchy, Pinchot thought it should be dammed and its reservoir used to provide drinking water to the people of San Francisco.

At the other extreme was naturalist and conservationist John Muir, who argued fiercely that loggers, miners, and dam builders were not managing a natural resource, but were instead actively destroying nature. When Gifford Pinchot and the California dam builders insisted on flooding Hetch Hetchy, Muir declared:

These temple-destroyers, devotees of ravaging commercialism, seem to have a perfect contempt for Nature, and, instead of lifting their eyes to the God of the mountains, lift them to the Almighty Dollar.

Dam Hetch Hetchy! As well dam for watertanks the people's cathedrals and churches, for no holier temple has ever been consecrated by the heart of man.[11]

Leopold would struggle all of his life with the question of what proper land management meant. He was torn between utilitarianism—using natural resources for logging, farming, grazing, and other human purposes—and conservation—or keeping nature pure and untouched by people. More and more, he would come to believe that there must be a balance between keeping the wild *wild* and taking advantage of its resources.

Graduation

In the spring of 1909, Leopold and the other thirty-four members of his forestry class were ready for graduation. In March, they left behind their books and classrooms, and sailed for Texas where they would have a final field assignment. Then each of them would join the U.S. Forest Service and be assigned to a different western national forest. Leopold was extremely excited. His dream was to rise up through the forest service to become a forest supervisor. One of his fellow students declared that "I'd rather be a [national forest] Supervisor than be the King of England."[12] In a letter, Leopold told his parents that he could not agree more.

3

The Great Forester

In 1891, Congress established the first forest reserves—government officials were concerned that uncontrolled logging would lead to a shortage of wood for construction projects.

By 1900, there were thirty-eight reserves encompassing 46 million acres. Under President Theodore Roosevelt, the system expanded rapidly. Roosevelt was the first enthusiastic conservationist to be president and he saw the national forest system not only as a way to provide wood for home building, but as a means for protecting wildlife and their habitat for the good of all the people. In 1905, he started the U.S. Forest Service and appointed forester Gifford Pinchot as its head administrator.

By the time Aldo Leopold headed for his first assignment as a national forest ranger, President Roosevelt and Gifford Pinchot had expanded the national forest system to an astounding 149 forests and 168 million acres. But that was just the beginning of the task ahead. Some of these forests were in terrible condition, having been heavily logged and overgrazed by cattle and other animals. Leopold and the other graduates from the Yale Forestry School had a great deal of work to do.

Greenhorn Ranger

Leopold was just twenty-two years old in 1909 when he arrived in the Southwest. He was assigned to some of the wildest territory in all of Forest Service District Three, which included the New Mexico and Arizona territories that had yet to achieve statehood. Leopold's first assignment took him to Apache National Forest, land that had been home to the Apache Indians just twenty-five years before Leopold arrived. It was a rugged territory, crisscrossed by steep roadless canyons and mountain ridges. The forest headquarters was a two-day stagecoach ride from the last railroad stop. The only method of travel into the forest was either on horseback or on foot.

Leopold's job was to preserve a perpetual supply of timber for industry and to help make decisions about grazing permits and water rights. Dressed like a cowboy, carrying pistols and a rope, and riding in the saddle of his stallion, Jiminy Hicks, Forest Assistant Leopold loved his work. "Why I wouldn't trade it for anything else under the sun," he wrote his mother.[1]

His day-to-day job consisted mostly of inspecting trees and marking them for cutting, and planting seedlings. The region was still mainly wilderness, and its ecosystem was largely intact. As a result, Leopold was able to get an up-close look at the relationships between predators like wolves and coyotes and game animals like deer, elk, and antelope.

The young foresters conducted a relentless war against the predators—wolves, mountain lions, and grizzly bears—and tried to exterminate all of them. It was during this time that Leopold shot the old wolf and watched the fire in her eyes die. Though he would not completely understand it for many years, something in him changed that day. From then on, Leopold began to alter his viewpoint: He came to view human beings not as better than, and above nature, but as an integral part of the ecosystem and on an equal footing with other creatures. He began to appreciate the value

The Apache National Forest was Leopold's first assignment as a forest ranger. The Apache and the Sitgreaves National Forests were administratively combined in 1974. The two million acre Forest encompasses magnificent mountain country in east-central Arizona along the Mogollon Rim and the White Mountains.

of every species and the role that each played in a healthy ecosystem.

Missteps

Things did not always go well for the young ranger. When Leopold was assigned to map the eastern edge of Apache National Forest and its trees, he was tripped up by his weakness in math and his inexperience as a leader. The men who worked for him found him to be disorganized and easily distracted by the urge to hunt down poachers or predators. When the project was completed, Leopold was ashamed to find that his altitude calculations were off by as much as one thousand feet, and he went two months behind schedule recalculating and correcting his errors. An investigation cleared Leopold of any wrongdoing, but it did show that he had a lot of growing up to do. Fortunately, Leopold did much better on later reconnaissance trips.

Promoted to Supervisor

In 1911, Leopold transferred to Carson National Forest in northern New Mexico. He was promoted to deputy supervisor, earning $1,400 per year. A little later he realized his dream and he was promoted to supervisor.

In these new positions, he was able to contrast the nearly pristine wilderness of Apache National

When Leopold became a forester in the American southwest in 1909, the only way in or out was on horseback. Leopold is shown here on his horse, Polly, in Carson National Forest in 1912.

Forest with the Carson National Forest, one that had been heavily used and abused by people. He was able to see for himself how illegal overgrazing by sheep and cattle could destroy the land and make it unlivable for wild game.

Leopold and his men worked to bring this illegal abuse to a quick end, canceling permits and

While working as a ranger in Carson National Forest, Leopold became very sick and nearly died after being caught in a storm. Though he recovered, he was never again as strong or healthy as he had been as a young man.

taking possession of livestock being grazed illegally in the forest. To do the job, he and his rangers rode the land with their guns at the ready.

Leopold took his first step as a professional writer by publishing the *Carson Pine Cone,* a newsletter that addressed national forest policy, provided conservation tips, and publicized doings in the Carson National Forest. He listed himself as chief editor, illustrator, and contributor.

Marriage and a Near-Fatal Illness

Shortly after he started working in Carson National Forest, Aldo Leopold met Estella Bergere in Albuquerque, New Mexico. Estella was a first-grade teacher. The two liked each other immediately, and a few weeks later, they went to a dance together. On October 9, 1912, the two were married. Over time, they would have five children: Starker, born in 1913 and named for his paternal grandfather; Luna born in 1915, Nina born in 1917, Carl born in 1919, and, finally, Estella born in 1927.

Aldo Leopold and his brother Frederic, who also worked for the U.S. Forest Service at the time, built a small house for the newly married couple. At first, everything went well for the Leopolds, but then, a near tragedy occurred.

Aldo and Estella Bergere Leopold, shortly after they were married in 1912.

On a forest service trip in 1913, Leopold was caught in a severe hailstorm. After days of riding in horrible weather, he finally reached home safely. But he became very sick and nearly died. He spent more than a year recovering from Bright's disease, or nephritis, an acute inflammation of the kidneys. The disease weakened him and he would never again be as strong or as healthy.

Sick and forced to stay in bed, Leopold read deeply about wildlife. He collected quotes, perhaps most notably Thoreau's: "In wildness is the preservation of the world."[2] He also read William Temple Hornaday's book, *Our Vanishing Wild Life, Its Extermination and Preservation,* which described the recent and alarming disappearance of many species, especially game animals, such as elk, deer, and ducks. The book declared that

we no longer destroy great works of art. They are treasured, and regarded as of priceless value; but we have yet to attain the state of civilization where the destruction of a glorious work of Nature, whether it be a cliff, a forest, or a species of mammal or bird, is regarded with equal abhorrence. The whole earth is a poorer place to live in when a colony of exquisite egrets or birds of paradise is destroyed in order that the plumes may decorate the hat of some lady of fashion, and ultimately find their way into the rubbish heap. . . .[3]

The preservation of animal and plant life, and of the general beauty of Nature, is one of the foremost duties of the men and women of to-day. It is an imperative duty, because it must be performed at once, for otherwise it will be too late. Every possible means of preservation—sentimental, educational and legislative—must be employed.[4]

Words of Warning

This warning made a lot of sense to Leopold. He had seen how wildlife had been decimated by the market hunters back home in Iowa, and in the eastern United States, as well as in the West at Carson National Forest. In Apache National Forest, he had also seen how an undisturbed and healthy ecosystem works. He worried that his children might grow up without knowing the natural beauties he had come to appreciate.

Leopold began to write articles for the *Carson Pine Cone* newsletter that urged his rangers to go out of their way to protect all resources in their jurisdiction, not just timber, but "water, forage, farm, recreative, game, fish and 'scenic' resources."[5] This was a resource list that went far beyond the Forest Service's official charter of protecting logging and grazing interests.

Leopold was forced to take a leave of absence from the Forest Service while he recovered from his illness. After spending almost eighteen months recuperating, the Forest Service gave Leopold a desk job in Albuquerque. It appeared that Leopold's days riding the range were over.

Winning Over the Public

In 1915, Leopold made a revolutionary proposal: He suggested that the forest service should manage game animals as vigorously and as scientifically as it did its trees. As Leopold saw it, the goal should be to restore populations of game animals that had plunged in recent decades. While Leopold only envisioned applying his plan in the Southwest, others in the service understood it as an important potential expansion of the National Forest Service's mission. Unfortunately, Leopold's visionary plan was rejected.

Leopold continued to press for his game management plan. When those within the forest service refused to listen, he went to the public. Leopold worked to establish game management associations all over the Southwest. He hoped that these local chapters of the American Game Protective Association would lobby government to start protecting and managing the herds of deer and elk. Leopold even invited his new hero, William Temple Hornaday, the author of *Our Vanishing Wild Life,* to speak at several game management rallies. Public pressure, often orchestrated by Leopold's writings, eventually led to the acceptance of his Forest Service game management mission.

Helping Save a Canyon

In 1915, Leopold became head of tourism and recreation for the forest service in the Southwest. In that role, he sought to protect the Grand Canyon from ruin. In 1903, President Theodore Roosevelt had stood on the edge of the Grand Canyon and declared:

In the Grand Canyon, Arizona has a natural wonder . . . which is in kind absolutely unparalleled throughout the rest of the world. I want to ask you to keep this great wonder of nature as it now is. I hope you will not have a building of any kind, not a summer cottage, a hotel or anything else, to mar the wonderful grandeur, the sublimity, the great loneliness and beauty of the canyon. Leave it as it is. You cannot improve on it. The ages have been at work on it, and man can only mar it.[6]

Theodore Roosevelt, the twenty-sixth President of the United States, did more than any other President to expand the national forest system. During his Presidency, Roosevelt preserved almost two hundred million acres of land.

Grand Canyon aerial view.

Leopold was stunned to find that Roosevelt's plea had been ignored. He found all kinds of inappropriate businesses at the canyon—bright electric signs marred the views, peddlers sold trinkets at the canyon's edge, garbage was scattered around campsites, and sewage flowed into streams that flowed into the canyon.

Leopold worked closely with Forest Supervisor Don P. Johnston to create a plan to protect the canyon better while still promoting tourism. The effort to balance tourism with conservation in federal parks continues today and follows the path that Leopold devised almost one hundred years ago.

Thanks to Leopold and others, the fight to protect the Grand Canyon proved very successful. It went from being a poorly protected forest preserve to being a better-protected National Monument in 1908. Congress expanded and upgraded the Grand Canyon to a national park in 1919, meaning it was then fully protected from development and commercial exploitation and given it full protection.

The Setbacks of World War I

When the United States entered World War I in April 1917, the nation's considerable resources were plowed into winning the war. At the same time, conservation was not a top priority. Instead,

⬆ Because so many troops needed to be fed during World War I, forest rangers were ordered to issue huge numbers of permits allowing cattle to graze on protected land. This was good for the war effort, but bad for the land.

forest service rangers joined the army and went to war, leaving the national forests undermanned. Leopold, weakened by Bright's disease in 1913, could not join the army.

The army fighting in Europe needed huge amounts of beef to feed it. As a result, Leopold and other foresters were ordered to issue huge numbers of cattle grazing permits on forest service land. While this aided the war effort, it was not good for the land. Leopold was so saddened that so many of America's natural resources were diverted to the war that he left the U.S. Forest Service in 1918. At the time he wrote: "The truth is that in spite of all religion and philosophy, mankind has never acquired any real respect for the one thing in the Universe that is worth most to Mankind—namely Life."[7] Leopold was saddened by the loss of human life in the war and also by the country's lack of respect for nature in a time of war.

And while men fought fierce battles in Europe, Leopold went to work for the city of Albuquerque, New Mexico, helping found a park along the Rio Grande and promoting tourism and road-building in the city.

A Return to the Forest Service

After World War I, Leopold happily rejoined the U.S. Forest Service as the second highest-ranking officer in the U.S. Southwest's District Three.

U.S. Army soldiers on their way to Europe to fight in World War I. When the United States entered World War I in April 1917, the nation's considerable resources went toward winning the war.

As assistant forester in charge of operations, he did excellent work documenting how overgrazing was destroying national forests in the region. More important, Leopold was a pioneer in pushing to have areas within the National Forest System declared wilderness areas, to be left wild and undeveloped. If people wanted to get "back to nature," Leopold wrote, the government ought to preserve "a little nature to get back to."[8]

Founding America's First Wilderness Area

Long before anyone else had considered such an idea, Leopold proposed that the U.S. Forest Service should set aside the Gila Wilderness as a preserve that would be maintained without human interference. Leopold was suggesting that the Forest Service expand its mission, that it should not just manage timber and grazing permits, but put aside vast areas of land that would be for wildlife only.

Gila Wilderness

In the autumn of 1919, Leopold patrolled the Southwest's remote Gila River on horseback. He was there to scout out a new road system that would be the region's first. Such a road system would open the area to logging and grazing. Adding roads would destroy the undisturbed habitat where wolves and mountain lions still hunted.

Then and there, Leopold resolved that there should be no road system. Instead, he sent out surveyors who defined the boundaries of a 755,000-acre-wild zone, that he proposed calling the Gila Wilderness. Within its boundaries there would be no buildings, no phone or electrical

The Gila River flows through the Gila Box Riparian Conservation Area in Arizona.

lines—and no roads. Wildlife would be allowed to run free with no interference from people. Human beings who entered the wilderness would have to do so on foot or horseback.

Thanks in no small part to Aldo Leopold, a few other Forest Service employees and the local community, on June 3, 1924, the entire 755,000 acres was set aside by the U.S. Forest Service as the Gila Wilderness. It was the first designated wilderness land in the United States.

[Today] The Wilderness areas on the Gila [River] comprise a vast, roadless realm astride the Black, Mogollon, Diablo, and Blue mountain ranges, varying from grassland foothills upward through juniper woodland, ponderosa pine, and spruce-fir forests on the high peaks. Mountain meadows, aspen glades, and spruce forests border on narrow, rock-walled canyons which in some places plunge to depths of more than a thousand feet.[9]

Today there are 702 federal wilderness areas in the United States, totaling 107,436,608 acres. Without the visionary and conscientious work of Aldo Leopold, there might be no wildernesses at all.

Last Years With the U.S. Forest Service

Leopold continued to make scientific surveys of the Southwest's national forests, studying how humans and nature interact. He came to recognize more and more that policies motivated by greed and industry were wrecking the forests. Too many trees were being cut, and too many grazing permits were being issued, a combination that resulted in terrible erosion. In many cases, wildlife and game were sacrificed to new roads, railroads, logging operations and ranches.

More and more, Leopold began to think radically. Influenced by the Russian philosopher Piotr D. Ouspensky, Leopold began to think of the entire earth as being like a living organism that demanded our respect. He began to imagine that the earth's parts—its oceans, landmasses, and atmosphere—work together much like the organs of a living thing. Leopold suggested that we should "respect [the earth] collectively not only as a useful servant but as a living being, vastly less alive than ourselves in degree, but vastly greater than ourselves in time and space—a being that was old when the morning stars sang together, and when the last of us has been gathered unto his fathers, will still be young."[10]

Leopold added that the reason "we can not destroy the earth with moral impunity," is because it is not dead but alive.[11] Such deep ecological thinking anticipated the thinking of scientist James Lovelock. In the 1960s, Lovelock outlined his controversial theory that said the earth and all its living and nonliving parts tend to act as a self-regulating organism. Lovelock's idea, called the Gaia hypothesis, remains an important tenet of the environmental movement.

Unfortunately, Leopold's thinking was more advanced than most national foresters, who thought that public land should be protected in order to provide people with timber. In 1924, increasingly seen as too rebellious and innovative in his thinking, Leopold was moved out of the Southwest and into a position as assistant director of the forest service's Forest Products Laboratory in Madison, Wisconsin.

Career Change

Leopold was not happy. He loved the Southwest, and he wasn't excited about moving his family to the tame Midwest countryside. The laboratory in Madison was where timber was tested to see how it might be made more useful to the public. It was a job particularly unsuited to wilderness-loving Leopold.

Leopold did not like desk and lab work and he missed hiking and riding in the field, but he did his job without grumbling. Field surveys to various national forests kept him sane and connected to his beloved outdoors. So did weekend camping trips with his wife and their four children.

Still Leopold thought he could make better use of his time. By 1928, he was looking for a new job outside the forest service.

The Nation's Ecologist

Aldo Leopold had been using the word *ecology* to describe his work since 1920, even though most Americans had never heard the word. *Ecology* comes from two Greek words: *oikos,* which means "house," and *logos,* which means "study." So ecology literally means the "study of a house."[1] The word was coined in 1866 by German scientist Ernst Haeckel who saw ecology as the study of species and how they relate to one another in their territory, or habitat.[2] By the time Leopold was forty years old, he was much more than just one of the nation's most innovative foresters; he was fast becoming one of the nation's foremost ecologists.

Leopold's Game Management Theories

In 1928, Leopold left the U.S. Forest Service and began private work assessing the nation's game lands. He went to work for the Sporting Arms and Ammunitions Manufacturers' Institute (SAAMI), a job that at first seems contradictory to his conservation values. SAAMI was, after all, an organization of gun and bullet manufacturers, as interested in shooting game as preserving it. But Leopold recognized that the future of SAAMI's businesses depended on scientific game management policies. After all, there would be no need for hunting rifles and ammunition if there were no deer or other game left to shoot.

Leopold eventually did game surveys in nine states. The work took tremendous commitment and energy. He traveled to each state, studied public records in detail, talked to scientists and game managers, birders and naturalists, politicians and foresters. And most important, he inspected the land.

One fact became overwhelmingly clear to Leopold: the destruction of habitat—the loss of forests, meadows, and wetlands—was bad for the game populations. The more human structures—roads, houses, and businesses—there were, the less game remained. More important,

Leopold found that small game refuges set aside for hunting were not very effective. If the surrounding countryside had been cleared of trees or paved over, then the game populations in these tiny refuges did not thrive. Leopold urged that more research be done to learn how to restore habitat in order to save and promote healthy game species. He wrote: "Why do species become extinct? Because they first become rare. Why do they become rare? Because of shrinkage in the particular environments which their particular adaptations enable them to inhabit. Can such shrinkage be controlled? Yes, . . . [t]hrough ecological research."[3]

By the start of the 1930s, Leopold's scientifically based game management policies had begun to take root around the nation, policies which he imagined could transform and protect the nation's ecology. In his important book *Game Management*, he wrote:

[T]wenty centuries of "progress" have brought the average citizen a vote, a national anthem, a Ford, a bank account, and a high opinion of himself, but not the capacity to live in high density without befouling and denuding his environment, nor a conviction that such capacity, rather than such density, is the true test of whether he is civilized. The practice of game management may be one of the means of developing a culture which will meet this test.[4]

The Great Depression

In 1929, the United States stock market crashed, leading to and launched the Great Depression. Millions of people lost their jobs and were forced to stand in long lines just to get food. It was a difficult time for the Leopold family too.

Fortunately, as the Great Depression worsened, Leopold was hired to work with President Franklin Roosevelt's Civilian Conservation Corps, or CCC. The CCC was started by President Roosevelt to give unemployed people jobs. It was

⬆ The Great Depression forced many Americans to depend on "bread lines" run by local charities. These lines helped feed many people who did not have jobs or money for food.

called Roosevelt's Tree Army, and its role was to help restore the nation's devastated forests around the country. Between 1933 and 1942, the CCC was credited with planting an estimated 3 billion trees.[5]

Leopold worked with the CCC, supervising erosion control across his beloved Southwest. He was appalled at what he saw. He found that foresters, game managers, range managers, and erosion experts often acted at cross purposes, counteracting one another's good work.

The Dust Bowl

Meanwhile, terrible environmental devastation appeared in ominous clouds of dried-out topsoil blowing eastward in the Dust Bowl—a series of catastrophic dust storms that swept across the American prairies in the 1930s, destroying farms and spreading huge amounts of dust over cities. Leopold argued that these events were not mere acts of God, but were caused by farmers who failed to use good land management practices. This was the same argument he had first put forward back in school, when he gave his speech about the reasons behind the decline and fall of the Spanish Empire.

At this time, Leopold gave one of his most important and impassioned speeches, speaking to the Southwestern Division of the American

◐ Shifting drifts of dust caused a farmer to abandon his home near Liberal, Kansas.

Association for the Advancement of Science in Las Cruces, New Mexico. He said:

Civilization is not . . . the enslavement of a stable and constant earth. It is a state of mutual interdependent cooperation between human animals other animals, plants, and the soils, which may be disrupted at any moment by the failure of any of them. Land despoliation has evicted nations, and can on occasion do it again. It thus becomes a matter of some importance, at least to ourselves, that our dominion, once gained, be self-perpetuating, rather than self-destructive.[6]

In other words, civilization is balanced precariously atop the environment. If a civilization destroys its environment—its wild animals and its forests—then it eventually destroys itself. Only respect for, and wise management of, the environment by a civilization can assure that civilization's long-term survival. And wise management is dependent on good ecological science and good land stewardship.

Classroom in the Wild

On June 26, 1933, Leopold was hired to teach at the University of Wisconsin in Madison, creating the nation's first graduate program in game management, and eventually, wildlife ecology.

He was not a typical teacher. He had no required textbooks for his class. He believed that the only way that his students could learn about habitat and wildlife was to experience them firsthand, to study nature intensely and continuously. This often meant long hours of being exposed to the elements, to rain and snow, cold and heat, while the students watched deer or prairie chickens.

The students were expected to show up to class with binoculars, wearing heavy boots, winter jackets, and rain gear, and to be ready at a moment's notice to go off into the Wisconsin forests, meadows, and swamps. And at a time when only men were thought to be eligible to become wildlife managers, he welcomed men and women to his courses.

Leopold insisted that his students study far more than the species of game that might interest them. He wanted students to observe what plants the animals ate in what season, what soils those plants grew in, and how much rain it took to nourish those plants. He didn't want his students to become specialists who focused on just one part of nature. He believed that the only way to understand nature was to observe every aspect of it. At that time, there were few books that could help the students with this work. He expected them to look at the big picture and see how all the elements interacted with one another.

Watching the Detectives

Leopold saw his students as detectives learning nature's secrets. "The real game is decoding the messages written on the face of the land,"[7] he said. He also taught ecology as if it were an outdoor sport. Though he also thought of ecology as very serious work, he urged his students to conduct "amateur exploration, research for fun, in the field of the land."[8] He was convinced that if too many plants and animals went extinct the earth's ecology would unravel and fall apart. Then the human economy would collapse, as would civilization.

A Professor of the Land

Leopold had many other responsibilities at the University of Wisconsin. He gave speeches and radio talks about soil erosion and game management. He conducted his own research into the history of Wisconsin birds and mammals and

Severe soil erosion left many fields on farms all across America looking like this.

Contour plowing, with furrows curved around the sides of a slope instead of straight up and down the slope, helped reduce both water and wind erosion by better retaining moisture.

looked for ways to improve the land to support these species. Working with local farmers, he created nationally recognized model programs for the conservation of game, the planting of trees, and the rehabilitation of worn-out soils. He helped farmers experiment with crop rotation, contour plowing, and strip cropping to prevent erosion. He taught them to fence off steep slopes from grazing livestock so that the slopes could revegetate. And he taught them to grow shrubs and trees on their land that would attract game, a technique called game cropping. Leopold also recruited high-school conservation groups to help him with his research, believing that people of any age can learn about and contribute effectively to scientific research.

The University of Wisconsin Arboretum

One of Leopold's most important jobs as professor was to help establish a new arboretum for the university (an arboretum is a place where trees, shrubs, vines, and other plants are cultivated for scientific and educational purposes). But the University of Wisconsin Arboretum was to be very different. "Our idea in a nutshell," said Leopold at the arboretum's 1934 dedication ceremony, "is to reconstruct, primarily for the use of the University, a sample of original Wisconsin—a sample of what Dane County looked like when our ancestors arrived here during the 1840s."[9]

From Theory to Reality

The site for the arboretum was a 245-acre run-down farm, purchased by the college on the shore of Lake Wingra in the heart of Madison. It took a lot of work to convert the abandoned farm into a thriving arboretum featuring native Wisconsin plants. The old agricultural land was gullied by erosion. Its soils had been depleted by years' of intensive agricultural practices. Many invasive species of weeds choked the land, making it uninhabitable for native plants and game species. Leopold saw the creation of the arboretum as an opportunity to put his ecological principles to work, and to see if his techniques of earth stewardship could help to heal and restore the land. The seeds of native plant species (those plants that had originally grown in Wisconsin before it was settled by the pioneers) were sought from all over the state and planted at the arboretum. Civilian Conservation Corps workers and volunteers battled to nourish and protect the young native plants during the intense drought of the 1930s.

Today, the University of Wisconsin-Madison Arboretum is a showcase of native habitats, and it is recognized as the birthplace of ecological restoration. The arboretum includes the oldest and most varied collection of restored ecological communities in the world, including tallgrass prairies, savannas, deciduous and conifer forests, and wetlands. Among the natural gems found there is the sixty-acre Curtis Prairie, the world's oldest human-restored prairie.

Roosevelt Asks Leopold to Help

The 1930s were a time of intense drought, which was very hard on waterfowl such as ducks and geese. Duck hunters called on President Roosevelt to help restore waterfowl populations, if possible. So in 1933, Roosevelt formed the Committee on Wild Life Restoration. He picked Leopold to be one of the committee's three members. Leopold and his partners were challenged to come up with a plan for conserving the country's wildlife, something no one had done before, or knew exactly how to do.

One member of the committee suggested that thousands of duck eggs be incubated at facilities around the country, and that when the baby ducklings hatched, they be released to the nation's flyways. Leopold realized that such a plan would not work—like all animals, ducks need places to live. He proposed that the government buy as much exhausted farmland as possible and then convert that land into wildlife habitat. The idea was to help nature heal itself and to restore the bird populations at the same time nature restored the land. The president approved Leopold's idea.

The result was the establishment of the National Wildlife Refuge system, a network of nationwide preserves that is credited with keeping many bird species from becoming extinct. Today the U.S. Fish and Wildlife Service manages 535 national wildlife refuges, plus 3,000 small waterfowl breeding and nesting areas, covering more than 96 million acres. There is at least one refuge in every state and one within an hour's drive of every major U.S. city. The refuges are home to more than 700 species of birds and 220 species of mammals, 250 reptile and amphibian species, and more than 200 species of fish.[10] The mission of the refuge system and the U.S. Fish and Wildlife Service today perfectly matches Leopold's original hopes: "[It] is to administer a national network of lands and waters for the conservation, management and where appropriate, restoration of the fish, wildlife and plant resources and their habitats within the United States for the benefit of present and future generations of Americans."[11]

Founding the Wilderness Society

While President Roosevelt's Civilian Conservation Corps did much to help conserve America's forests, some aspects of its work actually damaged ecosystems. One was the CCC's effort to build a skyline road. In order to meet the needs of tourists in motorcars, the CCC was chartered to build spectacular highways that traveled the tops of mountain ranges. One such highway is the Skyline Drive in Virginia's Shenandoah National Park, and another is the Blue Ridge Parkway in Tennessee's Great Smoky Mountains National Park.

Alarmed by the habitat destruction these roads were causing, a small group of citizens banded together to see if they could stop future highway projects and protect America's last wildernesses. This small group included famed wilderness supporters Bob Marshall and Benton McKaye, father of the 2,100-mile Appalachian

President Franklin Roosevelt's creation of the Civilian Conservation Corps during the Great Depression helped conserve America's forests. However, the CCC also created scenic highways through some of those same forests, frustrating conservationists like Leopold.

Trail (a hiking path running from Maine all the way to Georgia). On October 19, 1934, Marshall, McKaye, and several others called on Leopold to join them to form the Wilderness Society. Their goals were "to secure the preservation of wilderness, conduct educational programs concerning the value of wilderness, encourage scientific studies, and mobilize cooperation in resisting the invasion of wilderness."[12]

Robert Sterling Yard, another founder, expressed the purpose of the group best: "It is imperative that all friends of the wilderness unite. . . . There is just one hope of repulsing the tyrannical ambition of civilization to conquer every niche on the whole earth. That hope is the organization of spirited people who will fight for the freedom of the wilderness."[13]

The Value of Nature

Leopold had his own thoughts on the value of wilderness. He said "Our remnants of wilderness will yield bigger values to the nation's character and health than they will to its pocketbook, and to destroy them will be to admit that the latter are the only values that interest us."[14]

Today, the Wilderness Society is a nonprofit organization devoted to protecting the last great, unspoiled wildlands in the United States. It has, for example, worked long and hard to protect the

Arctic National Wildlife Refuge, fending off attempts by Congress and oil companies to drill for oil there. The Wilderness Society continues its efforts to "deliver to future generations an unspoiled legacy of wild places, with all the precious values they hold: Biological diversity; clean air and water; towering forests, rushing rivers, and sage-sweet, silent deserts."[15]

Focused Forever on Conservation

In an essay called "Engineering and Conservation" that he wrote in 1938, Leopold eloquently discussed the role of the ecologist. "[O]ur tools are better than we are, and grow better faster than we do," he said. "They suffice to crack the atom, to command the tide. But they do not suffice for the oldest task in human history, to live on a piece of land without spoiling it."[16]

Aldo Leopold's goal, his ultimate hope, was to help cultivate the science needed for people to learn how to live in harmony with their environment.

⬆ Attack on Pearl Harbor.

A Sand County Almanac and the Land Ethic

On December 7, 1941, Japan attacked Pearl Harbor in the Hawaiian Islands, and the United States went to war. With America's entrance into World War II, many of Leopold's college students at the University of Wisconsin went off to fight in Europe and the Pacific. Leopold's son Carl went too.

The professor now found time to write, and he began work on a small volume of personal essays that would culminate his writing life and help revolutionize the conventional wisdom about the environment. That book would eventually become *A Sand County Almanac.*

Leopold studied nature and did much of his writing at "the shack," a run-down and worn-out Wisconsin River farm that he and his family had purchased in 1935. For the rest of his life, Leopold

🜂 Leopold and his family bought this Wisconsin shack in 1935. Restoring it and the surrounding land became his life's work and the source of his groundbreaking book, *A Sand County Almanac.*

worked to restore the abused acreage of the farm, planting thousands of trees and enriching its soils, and much of *A Sand County Almanac* revolves around those activities.

Tracing the Seasons in Wisconsin

Whenever he spent the night at the shack, Leopold would wake up early in the morning so he could listen to the birds as they woke. He used a photographer's light meter to determine how much light there was when each species began to sing. He also tracked the blooming, blossoming, and waning of the plants on his land, noting when each species budded, flowered, and lost its leaves throughout the seasons. Likewise, he would track and watch the rabbits, deer, geese, and other animals that lived on or migrated through his land. He did this year after year, keeping detailed records in his journals.

Days in the Life

These journals became the basis for the first twelve chapters of *A Sand County Almanac*. The chapters were lyrical and poetic, but at the same time, they were an ecological, scientific retelling of the year on his Wisconsin farm.

In the chapter entitled "January," for example, Leopold recounted a mid-winter thaw during which he observed a meadow mouse racing across a skunk track. Another observer might have stopped there, but Leopold knew that the unusually hot weather had melted the mouse's snow tunnel that provided it with cover. The same day, Leopold described a rough-legged hawk sailing over the meadow and diving into the marsh, most likely to catch one of the mice. In this scene, Leopold shows the interaction of several natural forces—snow, sun, thaw, mouse, and hawk—and helps clearly demonstrate the interrelationships of ecology.[1]

In other chapters, Leopold addresses other ecological and environmental topics. In the month of July, for example, he celebrates the blooming of wildflowers, such as the rare native Silphium. He also notes with extreme accuracy how many fewer flowers there are in the city than in suburbia, and how many fewer there are in suburbia than on his old ruined farm. Leopold laments the loss of the wildflowers, lost to the march of civilization.[2]

The remaining chapters of *A Sand County Almanac* leave Wisconsin for the wilds of Illinois and Iowa, Arizona and New Mexico (where we hear the tale of the old wolf Leopold shot when he was a young man), to Chihuahua and Sonora in Mexico, and to Oregon, Utah, and Canada.

It is in the last part of the book that Leopold lays out his most revealing ideas about ecology.

The Land Ethic

Many environmentalists feel that the chapter called "The Land Ethic" expresses the core message of *A Sand County Almanac*. In that chapter, Leopold proposes that our society begin to value and use land differently. In "The Land Ethic" Leopold asks people to

quit thinking about decent land use as solely an economic problem. Examine each question in terms of what is ethically and esthetically right, as well as what is economically expedient. A thing is right when it tends to preserve the integrity, stability and beauty of the biotic community. It is wrong when it tends otherwise.[3]

Put simply, Leopold's land ethic maintains that people have a moral obligation not only to other humans but to animals, plants, soils, waters, and air that make up ecosystems.

In this chapter of *A Sand County Almanac*, Leopold gives a short but hopeful history of civilization. He uses slavery as an example of people's ability to change long-accepted habits. For thousands of years, people kept slaves, considered them property, and felt they had the right to treat or mistreat them in any way they liked. But, finally, people around the world and in the United States came to understand that slavery in any form is wrong, and it was abolished.

Learning From Mistakes

Even today, nature is not loved, cherished, or respected in the same way we love our families and friends. As Leopold wrote many years ago:

[O]ur bigger-and-better society is now like a hypochondriac, so obsessed with its own economic health as to have lost the capacity to remain healthy.

The whole world is so greedy for more bathtubs that it has lost the stability necessary to build them, or even to turn off the tap. . . .[4]

. . . We abuse land because we regard it as a commodity belonging to us. When we see land as a community to which we belong, we may begin to use it with love and respect.[5]

Leopold hoped that a day would come when the earth is valued in the same way we now value our human families. This concept, which Leopold called "the land ethic," has begun to influence not only environmentalists, but the courts and legislatures as well.

A Sudden and Unexpected Death

Sadly, *A Sand County Almanac* was Leopold's last word on the subject of ecology and nature.

On April 21, 1948, he woke up early as he usually did. He went outside and down to the marsh by the Wisconsin River, counted geese, and recorded the information in his journal. There was a large migration underway, and he counted 871 geese, a record.

That afternoon, the Leopold family smelled smoke. A small fire at a neighbor's farm had gotten out of hand and spread through dried leaves and small trees. Always a good neighbor and fearful that the flames would spread to his property and to the precious marsh, Leopold and his family fought the fire. He sent his daughter to call the fire department, and left his wife to stand guard while he went to the marsh to head off the fire. He carried a water tank on his back and used it to spray down the dried grass to prevent it from igniting. As he fought the fire, Leopold had a heart attack. He fell down in the grass and died, the flames passed over his body, lightly burning the field journal he kept in his shirt pocket.

Leopold Goes Home

Leopold's family returned his body to his childhood home in Burlington, Iowa, where he was buried in the Leopold family plot on a small hill between two white oaks and two white pines.

Albert Hochbaum, one of his friends, summed up Leopold's life:

Aldo Leopold was a Great American. Few men loved the land so deeply as he loved America; few who have loved the land have examined it so carefully; and few who have examined the land have been so articulate in detailing their discoveries. Aldo Leopold's discoveries and his philosophies are just as important to America as Benjamin Franklin's.[6]

Harry Russell, another friend, eulogized: "The cause of conservation has lost its best friend.[7]

Aldo Leopold's book was unpublished when he died. His son Luna took over the editing and *A Sand County Almanac* was published in the fall of 1949.

Aldo Leopold's Legacy

Leopold was many things in his life: a great forester, a wildlife ecologist and game manager, a noted writer, an environmental activist and supporter of wilderness, and an extraordinary teacher.

Writer Julianne Lutz Newton sums up Leopold's work:

Leopold fought to save lands from human reckless-ness and to help people prosper, generation upon generation. Motivating his career was an elementary, lofty hope: that a rising population of modern, technologically powerful humans would learn and practice ways of living that met their various needs yet at the same time kept the land healthy.[1]

Gila Wilderness in the South-western United States.

While there are no statues to honor Leopold, there are many monuments that attest to his achievements. There is the Gila Wilderness in the Southwest, and the millions of acres of wilderness now found all across the United States. There is the University of Wisconsin Arboretum, and thousands of other similar arboretums around the nation that preserve and present nature to the public as it existed before America was founded. There is also the National Wildlife Refuge system that harbors America's greatest wealth of wildlife. And, of course, there are Leopold's words and ideas, which continue to inspire environmentalists around the world.

Leopold's greatest legacy may have been as a teacher. He taught through his spoken words as a professor and his written words as an author. He taught us to think not just of each individual piece of the environment; he taught us to understand how all those pieces relate to one another, and how together, they combine to make something much bigger and more spectacular.

A Teacher for All Time

In the Indian parable of the elephant, six blind men encounter an elephant for the first time. The first feels the elephant's skin and says the animal is just like a wall. A second feels the tusk and says the animal is just like a spear. A third touches the trunk and says it is like a snake. A fourth puts his hand on the leg and declares the elephant to be most like a tree. A fifth touches the ear and says the elephant is most like a fan. Finally, the sixth touches just the tail, and declares the animal to be like a rope.

> And so these men of Indostan
> Disputed loud and long,
> Each in his own opinion
> Exceeding stiff and strong,
> Though each was partly in the right,
> And all were in the wrong![2]

Wide-Eyed and Open Minded

Leopold was not like these blind men—he saw all of nature, all of humanity, all parts of the ele-phant, all at once! And he understood that you could not value one part while hating another. You could not save one part, while destroying another. To his students he said:

The object is to teach [yourself] how to read land. Land is soil, water, plants and animals. Each of these "organs" of land has meaning as a separate entity, just as fingers, toes, and teeth have. But each has a much larger meaning as the component parts of the organ-ism. No one can understand an animal by learning only its parts, yet when we attempt to say that an animal is "useful," "ugly," or "cruel" we are failing to see it as part of the land.[3]

He also said:

Conservation is a state of harmony between men and land. By land is meant all of the things on, over, or in the earth. Harmony with land is like harmony with a friend; you cannot cherish his right hand and chop off his left. That is to say, you cannot love game and hate predators; you cannot conserve the waters and waste the ranges; you cannot build the forest and mine the farm. The land is one organism. Its parts, like our own parts, compete with each other and co-operate with each other. The competitions are as much a part of the inner workings as the co-opera-tions. You can regulate them—cautiously—but not abolish them.

The outstanding scientific discovery of the twen-tieth century is not television, or radio, but rather the complexity of the land organism. Only those who know the most about it can appreciate how little we know about it. The last word in ignorance is the man who says of an animal or plant: "What good is it?" If the land mechanism as a whole is good, then every part is good, whether we understand it or not. If the biota, in the course of aeons, has built something we like but do not understand, then who but a fool would discard seemingly useless parts? To keep every cog and wheel is the first precaution of intelligent tinkering.[4]

Making a Difference

Aldo Leopold proved that just one person can make a huge difference in the world. And each of us can follow in Leopold's footsteps: There are

Published after his death in 1948, Leopold's book, *A Sand County Almanac,* changed many people's ideas about the environment and nature. In it, Leopold calls on society to value the environment not as an economic resource, but as something of value in itself.

many opportunities for children to study and become foresters, wildlife ecologists, game managers, or teachers. There are countless locations, from nature centers to natural history museums to state and local parks that provide opportunities to learn about nature and where you can begin a journey toward becoming an environmental scientist.

The first step? Go for a walk and begin looking at the world as Leopold did. Walk outside and take a look at your house, and realize that everything in it—the walls and roof, the furniture, the appliances, toys, and books—come from nature. At the same time, realize that some part of nature had to suffer in order to provide you with each of those things, appreciate that nature has suffered and continues to suffer so that we can be comfortable.

As you go on your walk, look closely—no matter where you live, you will see signs of nature. Everything around you: the largest trees, the smallest ants, the robins and the mosquitoes, the sky above and the soil below, all are part of your ecosystem. There is so much to learn, but it is spread out before you, just as it was for Aldo Leopold.

Why Be an Ecologist?

When Leopold wrote *A Sand County Almanac* in 1948, the world was already what he called "a

⟳ Among the many aspects of nature Leopold observed closely at his Wisconsin farm was the migration of birds. Each year, he would watch and count the number and variety of birds, like the geese shown here, that made their way north or south as the season changed.

world of wounds."[5] The nation's great forests had been cut down to make way for cities. The nation's rivers and air were polluted. Game and other wildlife species had been greatly depleted.

The world today is in even greater trouble. We now know that our planet's more than six billion people are using the earth's natural resources faster than they can be replaced. Yet people continue to pollute the land, water, and air at an unprecedented rate. In addition, by burning fossil fuels like coal and oil, virtually all scientists acknowledge that we are changing the very climate of the planet, which in turn dramatically impacts things like sea levels and animal habitats.

Still, despite all the damage that people have done, there is hope. It will be difficult, but if we work together, we can help heal the planet. This is what Aldo Leopold said: "We shall never achieve harmony with land, any more than we shall achieve absolute justice or liberty for people. In these higher aspirations the important thing is not to achieve, but to strive."[6]

Careers in Ecology

What Do Ecologists Do?

Ecologists study ecosystems—forests, deserts, oceans, grasslands, rivers, and even cities—in every part of the world. They study the interrelationships and interactions between organisms and their environment, including people, plants, animals, soils, water, air, and climate.

What Kind of Jobs Can Ecologists Get?

Ecologists can be professors and teachers, technicians, research assistants, field scientists, administrators and program managers, consultants, activists, and writers.

Who Do Ecologists Work With?

Ecologists work in many different fields. They work with physical scientists, social scientists, policy makers and government office holders, land and environmental regulators, environmental activists, and computer programmers and statisticians to understand better how organisms interact with one another and with the environment in which they live.

What Skills Do I Need to Become an Ecologist?

Ecologists are people who are curious and creative and love nature. They are passionate and detailed observers, able to accurately record their results. They love science and the pursuit of scientific mysteries. They do not jump to conclusions, but they figure things out step by step.

Important Dates

1887—*January 11,* Aldo Leopold is born in Burlington, Iowa.

1904—Leopold travels east to attend Lawrenceville School in New Jersey.

1905—Enters Yale University's undergraduate program.

1906—Enters Yale Forestry School.

1909—Graduates from Yale Forestry School and takes a position as a ranger in Apache National Forest in Arizona.

1911—Transfers to Carson National Forest in New Mexico as deputy supervisor; later becomes supervisor.

1912—Marries Estella Bergere; they have four children.

1913—Stricken with Bright's disease, a kidney ailment, Leopold is bedridden for much of the year.

1915—Placed in charge of public relations work for the U.S. Forest Service in the Southwest; writes a highly successful tourism/conservation plan for Grand Canyon.

1918—Disgusted with the decline of conservation during World War I, Leopold temporarily leaves the U.S. Forest Service and goes to work for the city of Albuquerque, New Mexico.

1919—Returns to the U.S. Forest Service.

1922—Submits proposal to establish the Gila Wilderness that is approved by the U.S. Forest Service in 1924.

1924—Transfers to U.S. Forest Products Laboratory in Madison, Wisconsin.

1928—Leaves U.S. Forest Service and goes to work as a consultant conducting game surveys in nine states for the Sporting Arms and Ammunition Manufacturers' Institute.

1933—Returns to the U.S. Southwest to advise Civilian Conservation Corps on forestry and erosion issues. Later in the year, becomes a professor at the University of Wisconsin, in Madison. Appointed to the Committee on Wild Life Restoration by President Franklin D. Roosevelt; helps to create the National Wildlife Refuge system.

1934—Helps launch the University of Wisconsin Arboretum.

1935—Is one of the co-founders of the Wilderness Society.

1942—Begins writing series of essays that will become *A Sand County Almanac.*

1947—Submits *A Sand County Almanac* for publication.

1948—*April 21,* Dies of a heart attack while fighting a brush fire on a neighbor's farm.

1949—Son Luna completes editing *A Sand County Almanac,* and the book is published to critical and public acclaim.

Glossary

Bright's disease—Also called nephritis, an acute inflammation of the kidneys.

Civilian Conservation Corps (CCC)—The CCC was started by President Franklin Roosevelt to give unemployed people jobs during The Depression. It was sometimes called Roosevelt's Tree Army, because one of its jobs was to go around the country and restore the nation's devastated forests.

conservation—The protection of the environment, often today called environmentalism.

ecology—The branch of science that studies the habitats and the interactions between living things and the environment. This term was coined in 1866 by the German biologist Ernst Haeckel from the Greek *oikos* meaning "house" or "household" and *logos* meaning "study" or "knowledge." Ecology literally means the "study of household."

ecological restoration—The repopulating of a habitat with its native species in order to return it to a previous natural state undisturbed by modern humans.

extinct—No longer existing.

forester—One who is employed for the purpose of protecting and maintaining woodlands.

Gaia hypothesis—In the 1960s, scientist James Lovelock outlined a controversial hypothesis that said the earth and all its living and nonliving parts tend to act like a self-regulating organism.

game cropping—A technique in which shrubs and trees are added to barren lands in order to attract game.

herbivore—An animal that is adapted to eat primarily plant matter.

hypothesis—An assumption made in order to test its consequences.

market hunters—Hunters who hunt wild game to sell to the general public as food.

niche—In ecology, the unique role and place held within a habitat by a particular species.

omnivore—A species of animal that eats both plants and animals as its primary food source.

ornithologist—A person who studies birds.

taxonomy—The scientific discipline of naming and classifying organisms.

utilitarianism—A term applied in the early 1900s in which land was put aside or "protected" for the purposes of managed logging, farming, grazing, or for other human purposes.

wildlife ecologist—One who studies the interrelationships of animals with their environment.

Chapter Notes

Chapter 1. Learning to Think Like a Mountain

1. Aldo Leopold, *A Sand County Almanac* (New York: Ballantine Books, Inc, 1970), pp. 138–139.

2. Peter Matthiessen, *Wildlife in America* (New York: Penguin Books, 1959), p. 198.

3. William Yardley, "Alaska to Pay Pilots in Plan to Kill Wolves," The *New York Times,* March 22, 2007, <http://www.nytimes.com/2007/03/22/us/22wolves.html> (April 3, 2007).

4. Aldo Leopold, *Round River* (Oxford: Oxford University Press, 1953), p. 146.

Chapter 2. The Early Years

1. Marybeth Lorbiecki, *Aldo Leopold: A Fierce Green Fire* (Oxford: Oxford University Press, 1999), p. 9.

2. Ibid.

3. Curt Meine, *Aldo Leopold: His Life and Work* (Madison: University of Wisconsin Press, 1988), p. 35.

4. Lorbiecki, p. 26.

5. Ibid., pp. 27–28.

6. Meine, p. 37.

7. Ibid.

8. Ibid., p. 72.

9. Nina Leopold Bradley, from the Wisconsin Academy Review: vol. 44, issue 4 (Fall 1998), "Sand County: The Essence of Leopold's Thought," *University of Wisconsin—Madison* <http://digicoll.library.wisc.edu/cgi-bin/wiacrev/wiacrev-idx?type=HTML&rgn=DIV1&byte=398971&q1=&q2=&q3=> (April 3, 2007).

10. Meine, p. 77.

11. Edwin Way Teale, *The Wilderness World of John Muir* (Boston: Houghton Mifflin Company, 1954), p. 321.

12. Meine, p. 80.

Chapter 3. The Great Forester

1. Marybeth Lorbiecki, *Aldo Leopold: A Fierce Green Fire* (Oxford: Oxford University Press, 1999), p. 41.

2. Henry David Thoreau, "Walking," *The Thoreau Reader* (Atlantic Monthly, 1832), <http://thoreau.eserver.org/walking2.html> (April 3, 2007).

3. William Temple Hornaday, *Our Vanishing Wild Life: Its Extermination and Preservation* (New York: Charles Scribner's Sons, 1913), Project Gutenberg, n.d., <http://www.gutenberg.org/etext/13249> (April 3, 2007).

4. Ibid.

5. Lorbiecki, p. 58.

6. Theodore Roosevelt National Park, "Theodore Roosevelt," *National Park Service,* n.d., <http://www.nps.gov/archive/thro/tr_cons.htm> (April 3, 2007).

7. Lorbiecki, pp. 79–81.

8. Ibid., p. 90.

9. Gila National Forest "Recreation—Wilderness," *USDA Forest Service,* n.d., <http://www2.srs.fs.fed.us/r3/gila/recreation/recactivity.asp?activity=wild> (April 3, 2007).

10. Susan L. Flader and J. Baird Callicott, *The River of the Mother of God and Other Essays by Aldo Leopold* (Madison: University of Wisconsin Press, 1991), p. 95.

11. Ibid.

Chapter 4. The Nation's Ecologist

1. "Ecology," answers.com, n.d., <http://www.answers.com/topic/ecology-1> (April 3, 2007).

2. Susan L. Flader and J. Baird Callicott, *The River of the Mother of God and Other Essays by Aldo Leopold* (Madison: University of Wisconsin Press, 1991), p. 190.

3. Clay Schoenfeld, "Fifty years of Aldo Leopold's Game management," from Patricia Powell, ed., *Wisconsin Academy Review* (September 1982), University of Wisconsin—Madison, <http://digicoll .library.wisc.edu/cgi-bin/WI/WI-idx?type=div&did =WI.V28I4.CSCHOENFEILD&isize=text> (April 3, 2007).

4. "Roosevelt's Tree Army: A Brief History of the Civilian Conservation Corps," Civilian Conservation Corps Alumni, n.d., <http://www.cccalumni.org/ history1.html> (April 3, 2007).

5. Hillis L. Howie, "The Prairie Trek," from The Regional Review, National Park Service, vols. VI, nos. 3–4, March–April 1941, <http://www.cr.nps.gov/ history/online_books/regional_review/vol6-3-4e.htm> (April 3, 2007).

6. Marybeth Lorbiecki, Aldo Leopold: *A Fierce Green Fire* (Oxford: Oxford University Press, 1999), pp. 146–147.

7. Julianne Lutz Newton, *Aldo Leopold's Odyssey* (Washington: Island Press, 2006), p. 273.

8. Aldo Leopold, "What is the University of Wisconsin Arboretum, wild life refuge, and forest experiment preserve?" from William R. Jordan III, ed., "Our first 50 years: the University of Wisconsin-Madison Arboretum 1934–1984," University of Wisconsin—Madison, 1984, <http://digicoll.library .wisc.edu/cgi-bin/EcoNatRes/EcoNatRes-idx?type =turn&entity=EcoNatRes004006130004&isize=M> (April 3, 2007).

9. America's National Wildlife Refuge System, "Fact Sheets," U.S. Fish and Wildlife Service, n.d., <http://www.fws.gov/refuges/generalInterest /factSheets/> (April 3, 2007).

10. "America's National Wildlife Refuges," U.S. Fish and Wildlife Service, n.d., <http://www.fws.gov/ refuges/> (April 3, 2007).

11. Michael Frome, *Battle for the Wilderness* (Salt Lake City: University of Utah Press, 1974), p. 123.

12. Ibid., p. 124.

13. Aldo Leopold, from *A Plea for Wilderness Hunting Grounds,* "Development," *Outdoor Life,* November 1925, reproduced in *Aldo Leopold's Southwest* by David E. Brown, ed., and Neil B. Carmony, University of New Mexico Press, 1990, pp. 160–161, University of Texas at Austin, <http://gargravarr.cc.utexas.edu/chrisj/leopold-quotes.html> (April 3, 2007).

14. *Fundamental Sustainability—Protecting the Wilderness that Sustains Us*, Sustainability Law Blog, n.d., <http://www.sustainabilitylawblog.com/2009/02/fundamental_sustainabilityprot.html> (March 3, 2009).

15. Paul Johnson, "The Geography of Hope," from the Wisconsin Academy Review, vol. 44, issue 4 (Fall 1998), University of Wisconsin—Madison, <http://digicoll.library.wisc.edu/cgi-bin/wiacrev/wiacrev-idx?type=HTML&rgn=DIV1&byte=407267&q1=&q2=&q3=> (April 3, 2007).

Chapter 5. A Sand County Almanac and the Land Ethic

1. Aldo Leopold, *A Sand County Almanac* (New York: Ballantine Books, Inc, 1970), pp. 4–5.

2. Ibid., p. 48.

3. Ibid., p. 262.

4. Ibid., p. xix.

5. Ibid., p. xviii.

6. Curt Meine, *Aldo Leopold: His Life and Work* (Madison: University of Wisconsin Press, 1988), p. 523.

7. Ibid., p. 522.

Chapter 6. Aldo Leopold's Legacy

1. Julianne Lutz Newton, *Aldo Leopold's Odyssey* (Washington: Island Press, 2006), pp. 5–6.

2. John Godfrey Saxe, "Six Blind Men and the Elephant," about.com, <http://hinduism.about.com /od/hinduismforkids/a/blindmen.htm> (April 3, 2007).

3. Susan L. Flader and J. Baird Callicott, *The River of the Mother of God and Other Essays by Aldo Leopold* (Madison: University of Wisconsin Press, 1991), p. 336.

4. Aldo Leopold, *Round River* (Oxford: Oxford University Press, 1953), p. 146.

5. Ibid., p. 165.

6. Ibid., p. 154.

Further Reading

Books

Allen, Judy. *Anthology for the Earth*. Cambridge, Mass.: Candlewick Press, 1998.

Brown, David E. and Neil B. Carmony. *Aldo Leopold's Southwest*. Albuquerque: University of New Mexico Press, 1995.

Byrnes, Patricia. *Environmental Pioneers*. Minneapolis, Minn.: Oliver Press, 1998.

Dunlap, Julie. *Aldo Leopold: Living With The Land*. New York: Twenty-First Century Books, 1993.

Knight, Richard L. and Suzanne Riedel, eds. *Aldo Leopold and the Ecological Conscience*. New York: Oxford University Press, 2002.

Lorbiecki, Marybeth. *Of Things Natural, Wild, and Free: A Story about Aldo Leopold*. New York : Twenty-First Century Books, 1993.

Pringle, Laurence. *The Environmental Movement*. New York: HarperCollins World, 2001.

St. Antoine, Sara. *The Great Lakes: A Literary Field Guide*. Minneapolis, Minn.: Milkweed Editions, 2003.

Yannuzzi, Della. *Aldo Leopold: Protector of the Wild*. Brookfield, Conn.: Millbrook Press, 2002.

Selected Works by Aldo Leopold

Leopold, Aldo. *For the Health of the Land: Previously Unpublished Essays and Other Writings*. Edited by J. Baird Callicott and Eric T. Freygogle. Washington, D.C.: Island Press, 2001.

———. *The River of the Mother of God: and other Essays*. Edited by J. Baird Callicott and Susan L. Flader, Madison, Wisc.: University of Wisconsin Press, 1992.

———. *Round River: From the Journals of Aldo Leopold*. Edited by Luna B. Leopold. New York: Oxford University Press, 1972.

———. *A Sand County Almanac: With Other Essays On Conservation from Round River*. New York: Ballantine Books, 1970.

Internet Addresses

Excerpts from the Works of Aldo Leopold

Selected passages from A Sand County Almanac, Round River, *and other writings.*
<http://gargravarr.cc.utexas.edu/chrisj/leopold-quotes.html>

EEK! Aldo Leopold Father of Wildlife Management

Read all about the Father of Wildlife Management and his influence on conservation in Wisconsin
<www.dnr.state.wi.us/org/caer/ce/eek/nature/aldo.htm>

Index